Gilbert Stephen Bailey

The Great Caverns of Kentucky

Diamond Cave, Mammoth Cave, Hundred dome Cave

Gilbert Stephen Bailey

The Great Caverns of Kentucky
Diamond Cave, Mammoth Cave, Hundred dome Cave

ISBN/EAN: 9783743319431

Manufactured in Europe, USA, Canada, Australia, Japa

Cover: Foto ©ninafisch / pixelio.de

Manufactured and distributed by brebook publishing software
(www.brebook.com)

Gilbert Stephen Bailey

The Great Caverns of Kentucky

THE

GREAT CAVERNS

OF

KENTUCKY:

DIAMOND CAVE, . MAMMOTH CAVE,
HUNDRED DOME CAVE.

BY

REV. G. S. BAILEY.

———•━•━•———

CHICAGO:
CHURCH & GOODMAN,
51 La Salle Street.

CHURCH, GOODMAN & CUSHING, Printers.
JOHN CONAHAN, Stereotyper.

TO

MY DAUGHTER,

ALICE EULALIA,

WHO,

ON MY DEPARTURE FOR THE SOUTH

IN PURSUIT OF HEALTH,

REQUESTED ME TO WRITE FOR HER A

DESCRIPTION OF MAMMOTH CAVE,

THIS LITTLE VOLUME

IS

AFFECTIONATELY DEDICATED.

1. Entrance Stairs.
2. Rotunda.
3. Cleopatra's Needle.
4. Serpent's Head.
5. Grottos.
6. Main Avenue.
7. Mammoth Stalagmite.
8. Armadillo Stalagmite.
9. Leaf Stalactites.
10. Cascade.
11. Variety of Stalactites.
12 Ship's Keel.
13. Magnolia Flower.
14. Columns.
15 Diamond Spring.
16. Eviscerated Body.
17. }
18. } Grottos.
19. Lot's Wife.
20. Diamond Grotto.

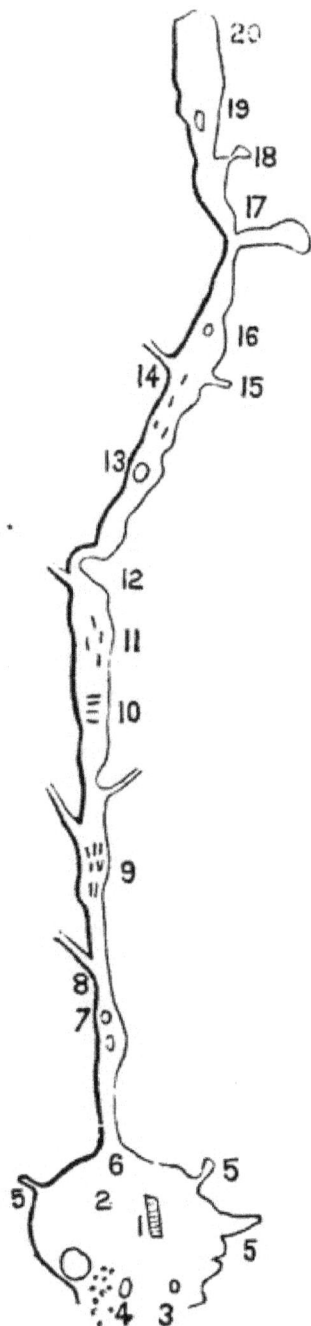

DIAMOND CAVE.

CHAPTER I.

DIAMOND CAVE.

The vast and beautiful caverns of Kentucky are justly ranked among the wonders of the world. During a tour in the South, in 1860, I availed myself of an opportunity to visit and explore three of the most noted ones, a description of which I will now attempt to give. These were the Diamond Cave, Mammoth Cave and the Hundred Dome Cave. They are near the Green River, in Barren and Edmonson counties, and all of them can be reached very readily by a ride of from two to eight miles from Glasgow Junction, a station on the Louisville and Nashville Railroad, about ninety miles south of Louisville.

I visited the Diamond Cave January 17, 1860. It is owned by Mr. Geo. M. Proctor. It was first discovered in July, 1859. It is sometimes called Richardson Cave, after Prof. T. G. Richardson, of New Orleans, one of its first explorers. It is situated less than two miles from Glasgow Junction, on the Louisville and Nashville Railroad, and about six miles from the world-renowned Mammoth Cave.

Accompanied by Mr. Proctor and several other gentlemen, we went in a hack a mile and a-half over gentle hills thinly covered with rather scrubby trees, until we reached a farm situated upon the gentle slope of a vast basin, which seemed some two miles across, the ground gently descending toward a common center, where the water which fell upon it gathered in a little pool, and eventually sunk through the crevices of the rocks.

About a quarter of a mile from the center of this great basin is the entrance to the cave.

It is in the midst of a smooth field, which could be cultivated up to the very mouth of the cave. The mouth originally was a mere crevice in the ground, which had to be enlarged by blasting before it could be conveniently passed. A small building has been erected over the mouth of the cave.

Entering the building, you find an abundance of lamps, and each visitor and guide takes as many of them as he can conveniently carry. You do not need to change your dress. You commence descending from the center of the building by a substantial stairway through the rock for forty feet. Here you land on a rocky floor. Now pause and look around and above you. You are in a magnificent rotunda, seventy feet in diameter and thirty feet high. Its form is somewhat irregular, but from the roof and sides is hanging a great variety of stalactites, from one inch to ten feet in diameter. These are formed by the dropping of water impregnated with the substance of

calcareous spar. From many of them the
water is gently dropping in winter and their
formation is constantly going on. But in summer, I am told, they are dry.

Passing behind the stairway you see a stalagmite rising from the floor five feet high and
six or eight inches in diameter, called Cleopatra's Needle. It is of a light brown color.
Near this, from the ceiling above, appears a
huge Serpent's Head, or rather upper jaw,
five feet long, two feet wide with stalactites
hanging from each side of the jaw like enor-
mous fangs.

Another immense stalactite hangs from the
ceiling, resembling a closed lily with the head
hanging down. This stalactite is ten feet long
and as large at the top as a sugar hogshead.

Most of the stalactites are covered with a
clayey oxide of iron which gives them a light
brown color, but some are white and clear as
an icicle. Various little alcoves or grottos
open in the walls at different heights, all rich-

ly studded with the most beautiful formations. Sometimes you see huge stalagmites encrusted with a kind of coral formation. It resembles petrified Irish moss.

Mr. Proctor, the owner of the cave, has built a substantial plank walk through it, raised from the floor and protected by railings. This precaution is taken in order to preserve its beauty. The floor itself is, part of the way, a bed of crystals which would be crushed and spoiled by walking on them. You pass onward, sometimes ascending and sometimes descending, through a varied avenue half a mile long, turning in almost every direction. Sometimes it is twenty or thirty feet wide, and then again just wide enough to allow you to pass, and from six to fifty feet in height.

Here and there are some openings which have not yet been explored, but all, as far as you can see, abounding with the most beautiful stalactitic formations. I cannot describe

the thousand wonders which everywhere meet
the eye.

There is that mammoth stalagmite, fifteen
feet high and twenty-five feet through, big as
a five ton haystack, one solid stalagmite, and
the largest one in the known world.

And then just by its side is the Armadillo
Stalagmite, which looks like a huge negro's
head, ten feet in diameter, and the *wool* made
of little globular stalagmites all over it, from
the size of a pea to that of a robin's egg.

The ceiling in several places is nearly white
and is thickly indented with holes half an inch
deep and the same in diameter. This is called the Vermiculated Ceiling. It looks some
like honeycomb, and some like a huge waffle
cake.

See those magnificent leaf stalactites of
every size, from an inch to ten feet in length;
some of them two or three feet broad at the
top, and from one to six inches thick. How
closely they hang together, so you can hardly

thrust your arm between them. There is that beautiful row of them, six or seven in number, and of graduated length, from four to six feet. Strike them gently with a stick and they give the different notes of a piano, according to their different sizes.

But here is the Cascade, not of water, but of magnificent stalagmites, in perfect imitatation of a cascade. You go down it by a good stairway and then look up. It is a succession of cascades for fifty or sixty feet in height. Those are not icicles hanging down there from the shelving rocks beside the falls, but stalactites, many of them six feet long and three or four inches through.

Pass onward through that great avenue full of all sorts of formations, some like icicles, some like a banner partly furled or drooping around its staff; some are like sheets through which the light of your lamp shines and shows beautiful colors. How they sparkle around you at times as if they were a mass of diamonds!

Now you see that great Magnolia Flower. It is six or eight feet long and four feet in diameter, hanging down from the ceiling. It is composed of stalactitic plates or leaves of calcareous spar, and strikingly resembles the magnificent flower of the Magnolia Grandiflora. You see around huge columns beautifully ornamented with cornices, moulding and curiously carved work. You find also several springs of water most delicious. There is a spring six feet long, two feet wide and a foot deep. The water is perfectly transparent, arched over with crystals, its sides and bottom a mass of glowing gems, which glitter through the clear water unobscured by any sediment.

But, having taken a refreshing draught from the spring, you pass on. Now put your lamp inside the hollow column of stalagmite which is somewhat larger than a man's body. You see every appearance of ribs, flesh, blood vessels and the red muscles, as the light shines through it. What strange resemblances these stones take! It surely looks like an eviscerated body.

Now you pass a grotto or two, and ascending a few feet, you see Lot's Wife, not a pillar of salt, but a beautiful, clear stalagmite about four feet high, and resembling a veiled female draped in white. You now come into Diamond Grotto, which is twenty feet in diameter and ten feet high. The floor is covered with crystals. Here you see innumerable forms of beauty which I cannot describe. The stalactitic formations here are of the most exquisite delicacy, many of them almost as clear as glass.

Returning now near the entrance of the cave, by a little circuitous route, you go below the floor of the Rotunda we first described. Passing now through a kind of Gothic archway, you enter a palace of crystals, with beautiful formations covering the ceiling, floor and walls. Stalactites and stalagmites abound everywhere, some reaching in slim columns from floor to ceiling.

You reluctantly leave this place and retrace your steps to the foot of the staircase which reaches to the mouth of the cave. Here, if you wish, you can step aside a few feet and see a mass of human bones, perhaps a wagon load. Was this beautiful place once the haunt of robbers, or was it not more probably used by the Indians for burying their dead, by throwing them down through the crevice of the rocks which formed the entrance?

Though the proprietor of this cave has established the excellent rule for the preservation of its beauty that no specimens shall be carried away, yet he was generous enough to give me some beautiful specimens for the cabinets of Shurtleff College and Chicago University.

This cave surpasses all others yet known in the exquisite beauty of its stalactitic and crystalline formations.

1. Entrance.
2. Pit.
3. Audubon Avenue.
4. Main Avenue.
5. Rotunda.
6. Church.
7. Gothic Avenue.
8. Post Oak Pillar.
9. Register Room.
10. Gothic Chapel.
11. Giant's Coffin.
12. Deserted Chamber.
13. Wooden Bowl Chamber.
14. Martha's Palace.
15. Richardson's Spring.
16. Side Saddle Pit.
17. Minerva's Dome.
18. Labyrinth.
19. Gorin's Dome.
20. Bottomless Pit.
21. Reveller's Hall.
22. Vale of Humility.
23. Scotchman's Trap.
24. Buchanan Avenue.
25. Fat Man's Misery.
26. Great Relief.
27. Bacon Chamber.
28. River Hall.
29. Dead Sea.
30. River.
31. Acute Angle.
32. Invalid Cottages.
33. Star Chamber.

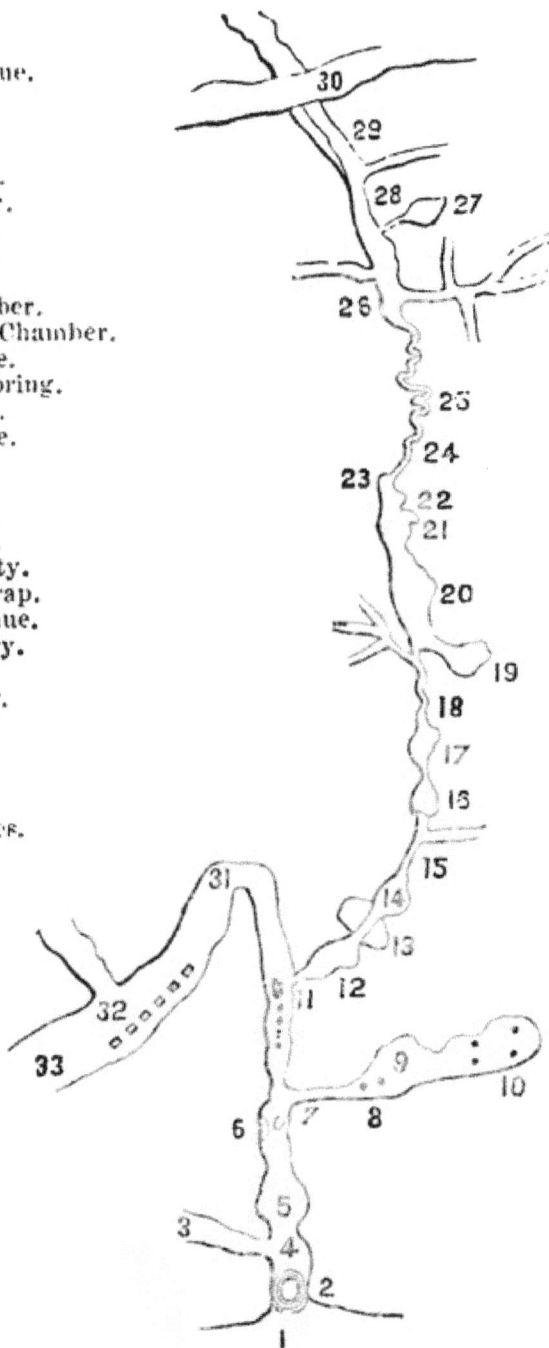

MAMMOTH CAVE.

CHAPTER II.

MAMMOTH CAVE.

I visited this one of the wonders of the world Jan. 18, 1860. Leaving Glasgow Junction on the Louisville and Nashville Railroad, at eight in the morning, I rode on horseback eight miles over wooded hills, which, in many places, were very steep and rocky. I passed but three or four houses on the route. The whole country around is made up of precipitous hills and vast basins which are deeply depressed in the centre. Some of them, not more than five hundred feet across from side to side, seemed to be one hundred feet lower in the centre than at the edge. Immense crevices at the bottoms of these basins permit the waters which are gathered by these great funnels to pass into the underground streams. No streams of water are found on the surface for miles around, except Green River, which seems to be the outlet of these subterranean streams. No creeks, brooks nor rivulets exist upon the surface, though the country is a constant succession of hills and hollows. The cliffs, the rocks by the road-side and even the small stones seem full of holes, recesses and grottos, as if all of them were trying to make little caverns in imitation of the great Mammoth Cave, just as children are prone to imitate the curious pranks and wonderful feats of older persons.

The Cave House was reached at ten o'clock. This is a large hotel kept by Mr. L. J. Proctor, for the accommodation of visitors. Soon as a guide could be called, and his lamps were ready, we started for the Cave. The guide is a negro, very gentlemanly and courteous in his bearing, full of wit, keen in his observations, and quite a philosopher you will think, as he gives you his theories of the various formations, the *hows* and the *whys* and *wherefores*, interspersed with true nigger wit and fun. He has an elegant command of language which would do honor to a member of Congress.

You descend a steep ravine for a quarter of a mile, and then turning a little to the right you are at the mouth of the Cave. This is a quarter of a mile from the bank of Green River, toward which the ground rapidly descends. The entrance to the cave is an opening in the side of the hill about 25 feet in diameter. You at once commence descending at an angle of 45 degrees, and go down about one hundred feet, keeping near the rocks on the right to avoid a yawning pit seventy feet deep right at the mouth. It is partly filled with the ruins of an old ice house once constructed in it, but which allowed all the ice to melt.

You now advance through a vast stone archway, in a wide avenue; passing a log cabin constructed within it for the preservation of fresh meat for the Hotel, you, in the distance of a few rods, come into the Rotunda, a vast room 100 feet across and 40 feet high. Here you see a countless number of common bats clinging to the ceiling by their feet, their heads downward, and so close together that you cannot see the wall between them. They are in a torpid state in winter, and in summer they leave the cave. This portion of the cave is aptly termed by some the *Battery*.

You now pass into the main avenue, which is about thirty feet wide. The walls and ceiling are of limestone rock, much of it nearly as white as a plastered wall. You leave Audubon Avenue to your left. It is half a mile long. We have not time to explore it.

As you pass along the main avenue you find large wooden vats sunk in the earth or among

the rocks, which once were used for leaching
the earth in the bottom of the cave to make
saltpetre for the manufacture of gunpowder
in 1812. Old pump logs lie along your path-
way through which they convey the liquid to
the mouth of the cave by means of a force
pump. The timber yet remains perfectly
sound. Here is also a cart road where oxen
and carts were used by the men of 1812. The
ruts are deeply cut in the rocks along the road.
The tracks of the oxen once made in the soft,
half-formed rock in some places, are now dis-
tinctly visible, the rock now thoroughly har-
dened around it. A pile of old corn cobs in
one place, your guide says, were left there by
feeding the oxen on corn in the cave. But
he gives you a cunning nigger laugh as you
suggest that he can easily replenish the pile
when antiquarians have carried away these
venerable relics—the corn cobs of 1812.

You travel over an irregular floor amid
piles of loose rocks scattered about. Some-

times the floor seems to glitter with crystals, and while you stop to pick up some imperfect crystals of quartz, your guide suggests that there are more *pints* than *quartz* there. But now under the edge of a shelving rock you find what seems to be petrified wood, the grains of which are very distinct. You soon come to the Church, a mere widening of the avenue, with a large recess for a pulpit and a shelving rock for a gallery. Religious meetings are sometimes held here by the crowd of visitors who resort to the cave.

You now come to the Giant's Coffin, a huge rock upon your right, some forty feet long and strikingly resembling a coffin. Here you leave the large avenue, and turning to the right around the foot of the Giant's Coffin, you go through a narrow passage down into the Deserted Chamber. This is simply a kind of room in the rocks. Entering another narrow passage, you proceed onward some rods and you reach the Wooden Bowl

Chamber, so called because its first modern explorers found in it a wooden bowl. Passing onward you soon descend a flight of wooden steps ten feet and you are in Martha's Palace, a beautiful room 25 feet in diameter, the ceiling of which is limestone, exhibiting various forms of beauty.

Passing around in a spacious avenue you find Richardson's Spring, a beautiful fountain of clear water, in a clayey basin right in the middle of the avenue. The water comes into it through a beautiful, smooth channel six inches wide, cut by action of the water into the soft rock and firm clay across the floor. The water is refreshing.

You now pass on through a beautiful archway of stone for several rods and come to the Sidesaddle Pit. It is right in your path and fifty feet deep. Going around the pit, you are soon in Minerva's Dome. This is about thirty feet high, and your guide here takes from his pocket a little package, lays it on a rock and sets the paper envelope on fire. In a moment you have a grand illumination. All the region round about you is brilliantly lighted for a minute or two, long enough for you to take a survey of the beautiful and grand objects around you. This is the Bengal light, made of pulverized saltpetre, sulphur and antimony.

Proceeding onward, you pass over rocks and soon enter the Labyrinth, a winding, narrow passage for several rods. Please excuse me for indefiniteness in stating the distance along these avenues and crooked passages. Leaving the Labyrinth you go down a flight of stairs, up another, then down again, and now you run up a little bye path and at the end you look through a hole in the wall, three feet in diameter, while your guide goes around to another opening and lights a Bengal light and illuminates a vast dome between you and him. You look downward till your head is almost dizzy but cannot see the bottom, for it is one hundred feet deep; and then you look upward one hundred feet to the top, if your nerves are steady enough to allow you to put your head through the hole far enough to get a full view. This is Gorin's Dome, one of the grandest sights in Mammoth Cave.

Return from this bye path now and pass on, and be careful, for here yawns the Bottomless Pit, right at your feet. Your guide lights a Bengal light and throws it down the Pit. As it sinks down and down it becomes less and less until it looks only like a star. He throws down a stone, while you hold your watch and count three seconds or more before you hear it splash in the water beneath, indicating a depth of at least one hundred and fifty feet. An iron railing prevents any special danger of falling as you pass along its brink. You now pass over the Pit on a wooden bridge and take a view of Shelby's Dome, a vast cavity above you and immediately over the Pit. Going soon onward, you soon reach Reveller's Hall, an expansion of the avenue, with a tolerably smooth floor, where parties sometimes stop for a dance, hence the name. But as you leave Reveller's Hall you soon enter the Valley of Humility, as all revellers should. Here you must bend or creep, for the passage is only about three feet high for several rods. But you come out among rough piles of rocks.

Here is the Scotchman's Trap, a triangular stone eight feet across and a foot thick, standing on one edge and leaning over a hole beneath, through which you must pass. The apex of the trap is caught against a point of projecting rock in the ceiling above and is thus prevented from falling and closing the passage. As your guide descends through the hole beneath the trap, he repeats the poetic couplet,

"The Scotchman's Trap is set by a trigger,
And if it should fall it would catch a poor nigger."

Whether you admire his poetry or not you must follow him through the Trap with the interesting feeling that you are liable to be caught there yourself as well as the "poor nigger."

But you have now reached Buchanan's Avenue, whose height requires you to lop your head a little, as it is said President Buchanan does; hence the name. Onward again and you are soon in the Winding Way, which leads to Fat Man's Misery, a mere crevice a foot wide, through which you must edge along for half a dozen rods. This will make you sweat if you have much of a corporosity. But squeeze along and you will soon come to a wide avenue, which you will think is rightly named, The Great Relief. Here you stop to rest a little and take a few long breaths.

You can pass on now at your leisure. Soon you see overhead encrusted in the ceiling the Odd Fellow's Links, a stalactitic formation of three links, about six feet long altogether.

You now enter River Hall. You turn aside to the right to explore Bacon Chamber, where the ceiling looks precisely as if it was thickly hung with hams in whitewashed bags. But they would be hard eating, for they are solid stone. Near these hams is a perfectly round cavity over head like a potash kettle thrust into the ceiling bottom up.

Now you proc. ed toward the River which runs through Mammoth Cave. You go over a muddy shelf of rock from which the high waters of the river have recently receded. Heavy rains the last few days have made a sudden rise in the river of twenty or thirty feet in perpendicular height. On your left, and fifteen or twenty feet below you, lies the Dead Sea, in which the water is now twenty-five feet deep. Look to your footing, or from your slippery path you may tumble into it.

Creeping carefully along you come to the river, which is now so high that the ceiling over its channel is still immersed several feet under the surface of the water. You cannot cross it until the water subsides. Nor can you catch any of the eyeless fish which abound there; but in the summer you may get them. They are white, and from two to seven inches in length. They are sometimes found in springs in the mouth of caves in this vicinity, and sometimes are drawn up in the well-buckets of citizens. The river in Mammoth Cave, at an ordinary stage of water, is about forty feet wide and twenty-five feet deep, and doubtless issues into Green River. The eyeless fish are sometimes found in this part of Green River, and doubtless come from the Cave.

You may now retrace your steps until you reach the Giant's Coffin. Leaving the Coffin again, you proceed onward in the main avenue. At the distance of a quarter of a mile you turn to the left, making an acute angle. The avenue is fifty feet wide. The air is pure, and you feel quite at your ease after

squeezing through the difficult passages in
the other part of your route. Onward for
another quarter of a mile and you pass some
little stone cottages, erected by men within
the cave about seventeen years ago, where a
dozen consumptive persons resided, by order
of their physicians, for several months. But
all of them eventually died of consumption.
Passing the cottages, you after a while see
the lofty ceiling, black in places, like clouds
in the sky. Soon it looks dark as if a heavy
storm was gathering above you, and at length
the sky seems entirely overcast. You are
now in the Star Chamber. Put your lights
away or blow them nearly all out, and look
up to the roof sixty or seventy feet high.
How intensely dark! But now you see the
stars glimmering from the roof. They are
whitened points of rock projecting through
the blackened gypsum which covers the ceiling. The Star Chamber is truly magnificent.

You now return to the Coffin again, and

pass it and proceed in the direction of the mouth of the cave. But you leave the main avenue by ascending a flight of steps to your left, fifteen feet high, and enter Gothic Avenue. Passing onward for a dozen rods, you see the Post Oak Pillar, a stalactitic formation as large around as your body. Onward some rods further you are in the Register room, a vast widening of the avenue, whose walls and ceiling are covered with the names of visitors.

Proceeding still onward, you reach the Gothic Chapel. Here are the principal stalactites of the cave. You see the Pillars of Hercules, Cæsar's Pillar, Pompey's Pillar and the Pulpit, all magnificent stalactitic formations reaching from the floor to the ceiling, some ten feet high, and from two to ten feet in diameter. From the ceiling are hung a multitude of stalactites from an inch to four feet in length. The finest ones have evidently been broken off and carried away as specimens, and the cave has thus been robbed of much of its beauty.

It is related that a couple were married in the Gothic Chapel a few years ago. The mother of the bride having told the daughter she hoped she would never marry that man upon the face of the earth, she concluded to marry him under the earth.

You now return to the mouth of the cave, having travelled some seven or eight miles, so says your guide. There are, however, beauties and wonders beyond the river which will richly reward you for another day's explorations when the water of the river is low enough to permit you to cross. Your guide can furnish you with beautiful specimens of satin gypsum obtained from the other side, and also some of the eyeless crawfish which he has caught.

But you have now seen one of the wonders of the world. As to its vast extent, it is unsurpassed. Its avenues, all combined, are more than a hundred miles in extent. But you are willing to leave the remaining ninety miles for some other day's explorations. By this time your stomach, also, feels cavernous and your jaws carnivorous, and you are strongly inclined to explore the dining-room of the hotel, and then seek an easy place to rest your wearied body. But your thoughts have found food for many days.

1 Entrance.
2 Reception Hall.
3 Spring Avenue.
4 Return Av.
5 M. Antony's Pit.
6 Coral Reef.
7 Grand Entr. Av.
8 Wall Street.
9 Ladies' Av.
10 Canada Hall.
11 Hill of Science.
12 Flora's Wreath.
13 Falstaff's Punishment
14 Broad Way.
15 Dripping Dome.
16 Court's Avenue.
17 Ocean Wave.
18 Pine Apple Avenue.
19 Elephant.
20 Vineyard Avenue.
21 Grape Vine.
22 Cabinet.
23 Twin Domes.
24 Cupid's Fountain.
25 Echo Avenue.
26 Dome Avenue.

27 Everett's Dome
28 Clay's Dome.
29 Mammoth D.
30 Canopied Pit.
31 Eureka Dome.
32 River Avenue.
33 Temple.
34 Ohio Monument.
35 Franklin Monum't.
36 Falls of Minnehaha
37 River.
38 Fairfield Avenue.
39 Kentucky Dome.
40 Punch's Trials.
41 Vulcan's Anvil.
42 Crystal Rocks.
43 Mollie's Boudoir &
     Bailey's Dome.
44 Natural Bridge.
45 Washington Monu-
     ment.
46 Irving's Monum't.
47 Kanes' Dome.
48 Alpine Pass.
49 Fluted Dome.
50 Prison Hall.
51 Nellie's Chamber.
52 Gibbon's Rest.
53 Ruins of Palmyra.
54 Duncan's Avenue.
55 Boone's Monum't.
56 Cathedral.
57 Vestry.
58 Black Donald's Pit.
59 Wool's Avenue.
60 Capitola's Trap.
61 Hurricane Avenue.

HUNDRED DOME CAVE.

CHAPTER III.

HUNDRED DOME CAVE.

This cave is one of the grandest, in its subterranean scenery, of any yet known. Though not so extensive as Mammoth Cave, yet it will take you an entire day, or more, to explore its vast avenues, its magnificent domes, and examine its beautiful and varied formations.

The entrance of this cave has long been known, but its extent and grandeur have remained unrevealed until October, 1859, when a young man of highly appreciative mind, and of dauntless courage and skill for such explorations, Mr. Kellion F. Peddicord, undertook and prosecuted his researches here for several weeks. His labors were rewarded with the discovery of some of the finest and grandest scenery of its kind that has yet been brought to human view.

Through the polite invitation of its first explorer, Mr. Peddicord, and J. D. Courts, Esq., the owner of the cave, I visited it January 19th and 23d, 1860. Leaving Glasgow Junction, on the Louisville and Nashville Railroad, in Barren County, Kentucky, about ninety miles south of Louisville, you ride for a mile over a smooth, level road, and then as you approach the house of Mr. Courts, the proprietor of the cave, you turn to the right and gradually ascend a rocky hill covered with its native forest for about half a mile; and then descending a few rods, you are at the mouth of the cave. The entrance is about half a mile from the top of the hill.

The opening is about fifteen feet in diameter. As you enter the cave, you descend a slope of forty-five degrees, for about eighty feet, when you stop in Reception Hall. This is a grand rotunda, fifty feet in diameter, and fifty feet high. Here you look around you with wonder and admiration. Just at your right, and projecting from the side of the rotunda, is Solomon's Throne, a magnificent collection of stalactites, hanging like curtains and drapery from the height of twenty feet, and reaching to the floor. They hang from the edge of a shelving rock, scolloped at the edge, the scollops from one to four feet in diameter, so as to give it a most beautiful appearance. Your guide goes behind and among them, and as the light of his lamp glitters among the stalactites, you have a most beautiful sight.

Turning now to the left of the entrance, you see the Genii's Retreat. This is a splendid formation of stalactites, looking like a series of cascades, descending from the height of thirty feet to the floor. Passing between the stalactites near the floor, you enter a little grotto eight feet in diameter, and you are surrounded with the most exquisitely beautiful formations.

Just beyond the Retreat, in the left hand corner of Reception Hall, is Jackson's Niche, a recess six feet wide and forty or fifty feet high. In the corner of Jackson's Niche is a succession of shelves some forty feet high, and fringes of stalactites hanging from each shelf. Near the foot of this is the Hermitage, a beautiful little grotto, made entirely of stalactites. Looking to the top of the wall opposite to the entrance of Reception Hall, you see a number of Epaulettes, a foot in diameter, the fringes being of stalactite. Near the foot of Solomon's Throne is a broken stalagmite, six or eight feet through, nearly globular, which has apparently fallen from the adjacent rocks.

From Reception Hall five avenues lead off in different directions. You take Spring Avenue, and soon you find a stream of water,

large as your arm, pouring from a crevice
eight feet above you, down into a wooden
trough, which was placed there in 1812, by
the men who manufactured saltpetre in the
cave. You pass on through a large archway
twelve feet wide, and six to ten feet high.
The ceiling sometimes looks as if whitewashed, and indented with little holes like a
waffle cake. Over your head are hanging
countless numbers of bats in a torpid state,
thousands in a group. You find elegant
formations of rock up this avenue for half a
mile. But you return to Reception Hall.

Now start again. You go over some loose
rocks, climb up about six feet, and enter Return Avenue. This at first is low, and you
must stoop or crawl. But you soon come to
quite a room. Here are Corinthian Columns
of fluted limestone seven feet high. Now
look off to your right. There is a horizontal
crevice, a foot or two high, and extending
indefinitely in width. Put your lamp in it.

You see the Coral Reef. This is a calcareous ruffle, standing up from the rock six inches high and one or two inches thick, and reaching in varied and beautiful convolutions for rods in extent, and as far as you can see. Small and delicate stalactites are hanging from the upper wall, all over the region of the Coral Reef. Two avenues lead off from this room, but we shall return again to Reception Hall.

You now go down through a hole in the rocky floor on one side of Reception Hall, and you are in Grand Entrance Avenue. Proceeding onward for fifteen or twenty rods, and passing the opening of an avenue or two, you come to Wall Street, a narrow and crooked channel through the rocks. Go up this some twenty rods and turn to your right into Ladies' Avenue. You now gradually ascend through most beautifully decorated walls, hanging with clusters which look like clusters of grapes. Going onward some

thirty or forty rods, you reach Canada Hall.
In it stands, or rather hangs, Brock's Monument, a huge column of smooth limestone.

Here you can easily inscribe your name on
the soft stone wall, using a nail for a pen.
While you are cutting your name, your guide
has gone up the Hill of Science, and holding
up his lamp, he calls to you to look. There
he is on the side of the rock twenty-five feet
high, at the top of what seems a waterfall
of stone. Ten feet above his head is Flora's
Wreath of stalactites.

Return now to Wall Street, and try your
skill through Falstaff's Punishment, for about
six rods. If you are as fat as Sir John you
may share in the punishment, for you enter a
narrow, crooked channel in the rocks where
you must get along edge-wise. Wo to the
fashionable ladies' hoops that go through
there! But now you are in Broadway, and
here is Dripping Dome, one hundred feet
high and fifteen feet in diameter at the base,

a cavity that might contain a large church steeple. The sides are of elegantly fluted limestone.

Immediately under this dome is Kellion's Pit, thirty feet deep, into which my guide, the first explorer of this region, fell in one of his earliest excursions. It was named after him; and it was a wonderful providence that he did not lose his life. By the assistance of his brother he was soon extricated but with a severe cut in his head.

All along Broadway are beautiful incrusta tions of alabaster, covering the rocks with a thin shell, from the thickness of paper to an inch or two. You can peel off yards of it, and tons of it are lying along the avenue which have fallen from the rocks above.

Now take Court's Avenue to the right. The walls are covered with little globules of marble attached to the rocks by a slender stem of stone an inch or two long. You soon come to the Ocean Wave, which rise:

from the floor of the avenue like the Coral Reef, only the stone ruffle rises a little higher. As you proceed up this avenue a few rods these ruffles cross the avenue at regular intervals like railroad ties, and you suggest to a good humored slave-holder by your side that this must be the terminus of the underground railroad.

Return now to Broadway, and proceed along it thirty or forty rods. The walls are covered with beautiful incrustations. You now see the Elephant, a huge rock partly projecting into your path, and about twice the size of an elephant and considerably resembling one. Passing this you turn to the left and enter Vineyard Avenue, which meanders among most beautiful formations of rock and incrustations.

Look at that magnificent grapevine, unequalled in beauty and perfectness of resemblance to a grapevine loaded with clusters of grapes. But the grapes are of calcareous

spar. The clusters hang closely grouped together in a mass as large around as a barrel.
This mass of clusters rises from the floor, at-
taches itself to the wall, and when it is a
little above your head, it extends off horizon-
tally as if lying over a tree-top.

Beyond the Grape Vine the avenue is called
the Cabinet, because it is full of such a
variety of formations. Look at that Golden
Pillar at your right. Now sit down on a
rock and pick up some of those ugly, round-
ish, white looking stones at your feet. Some
are as big as a hen's egg, others as large as
your fist. Lay one on a rock and break it
open with another stone. Is not that fine?
It is hollow, and the cavity is studded with a
perfect bed of diamond-shaped, transparent
crystals. These Geods will be elegant things
on your parlor table or in a cabinet.

Now return to near the Grape Vine, and
turn to your right through a crevice which
will just admit your body. Now you are in

the Twin Domes. The first is fifteen feet in diameter, of uniform size, and sixty feet high. Now pass through a little Gothic passage which requires you to stoop, and you stand in the other Dome. Its base is elliptical, eight by fourteen feet, and the Dome rises to the height of over two hundred feet.* The sides are of fluted rock, and down the side drips Cupid's Fountain; the water is caught in a projecting basin of stone just high enough to drink from, and is delicious.

Return now to the Elephant, and start out through Echo Avenue, a winding archway, where your footsteps ring and your voice sounds very loud. As you strike the floor with your cane it sounds hollow beneath, as if you could easily break through into unknown regions below. Who knows but

---

* For distances and heights, I rely on the estimates of Mr. Peddicord, the explorer of this cave, who is a practical engineer, and whose accuracy I saw no reason to question.

you are treading upon the thin coverings of vast domes below you, hundreds of feet deep? But you pass safely on amid the rocks beautifully formed into cornices and mouldings.

Now the avenue divides. You take the right hand one. This is Dome Avenue. You descend a few steps. What niches are cut out by falling water, though now dry. They look as if made for the reception of statues. But now you are in Everett's Dome, fourteen feet in diameter, and some three hundred feet high.

Now climb a ladder twelve feet high, go through a passage in the rocks, a few feet, and you are in Clay's Dome, sixteen feet in diameter, and as high as Everett's. Leave this high perpendicular crevice, and go a few feet, to a ladder, down which you descend twenty-six feet.

Now you are in Mammoth Dome. This is twenty feet across at the bottom, and tapers gradually to the top. Its height, who knows how much! If its diameter were a little greater you might put Bunker Hill Monument inside of it, and top that off with a tall church steeple, and from the top of that you might perhaps see the top of the dome. But your guide has sought out passages through the rocks until he has, a few weeks ago, come into the dome some four hundred feet from its base, and fixed a pulley there, by means of which he now raises a lamp through that magnificent cavity. Up and up, and still up it goes, until it is like a star in the sky. The height of this dome is probably five hundred feet. Some say it is more. Who will describe it? I cannot.

CHAPTER IV.

HUNDRED DOME CAVE.

(CONTINUED).

But pass on. You descend among some rocks. Do not fall into Canopied Pit, for it is right in your path, and twenty-eight feet deep. You are now in the midst of Grecian columns, and as you pass on and rise a few feet you are among beautiful stalactites hanging like fringes from the edges of the rocks. They are from an inch to a foot in length.

You now descend a ladder thirty-five feet, and are in the bottom of Eureka Dome. The floor is elliptical, nine by thirty feet, and the dome as high as the Mammoth Dome, higher than you can see with your best lights.

Its walls are rugged upon one side, smooth on another, and fringed and draped with stalactites on another. Now raise your voice and sing Old Hundred with the Doxology,

"Praise God from whom all blessings flow."

What grandeur and impressiveness are given both to the tune and the words, as they roll up through the vast domes, ringing and reverberating in those rocky tubes like grand organ pipes five hundred feet long! Returning now to Mammoth Dome, you stop and sing,

"When I can read my title clear,"

and now more than ever before are impressed with awe and reverence amid these sublime works of your Creator.

You now pass down a ladder twenty-eight feet into Canopied Pit. From its base you go through a low, Gothic passage into River Avenue. Here is a shallow pool of water only a few inches deep, and clear as crystal. There, catch that big crawfish, wrap him in your handkerchief and put him in your pocket. He is one of the natives of this region, white as milk. Not the sign even of an eye has he. What does he want of eyes here, a thousand feet below the surface of the ground and a mile or two from daylight?

Look up and you see the Temple, and the door, a thin slab of stone standing out from the wall like a door, and closing the entrance to the Temple. Pass onward a few feet, and you see Ohio Monument, a massive column of smooth limestone rock, twenty feet high and six feet through. On the other side of the room is Franklin's Monument, like the Ohio.

Enter another avenue and in a few steps you are at the Falls of Minne-ha ha. This is a little stream pouring down into a clear pool eight feet across, which you see through a wide crevice in the floor beneath you, while the falls and stream are out of sight, though they are plainly heard.

Returning to Echo Avenue, you enter Fairfield Avenue, and you are almost immediately in Kentucky Dome, twenty feet across and about two hundred feet high. I must not stop to describe each minutely. But here is grandeur and sublimity of scenery under ground which it is impossible to conceive without seeing it.

You now go down a gradual descent, through Punch's Trials, a narrow, crooked passage, though not difficult. There is Vulcan's Anvil sticking out of the rock, and a calcareous projection near it like a hanging lamp. The rocks are here covered with crystalizations which sparkle like gems. It is a kind of crystal net-work, like the delicate needles of ice which form on water when it begins to freeze over.

Proceeding along a winding passage some forty rods, you reach Molly's Boudoir, a beautiful room, over which rises Bailey's Dome, about two hundred feet high; from the top of which falls a spring of pure water into a pretty basin below. Now descend a ladder eighteen feet and you are on the Natural Bridge, which crosses over St. Patrick's Tomb, a large cavity beneath. On your left rises Washington's Monument, a grand column one hundred feet high. On your right is Irving's Monument, about equal to Washington's.

Now descend a ladder twelve feet and you are in Kane's Dome, two or three hundred feet high. Here you can enter St. Patrick's Tomb, and crack open more of those beautiful Geodes, full of crystals. But now climb that ladder eight feet, and soon another nineteen feet, and you are in the Alpine Pass. Go on for one hundred feet and then descend thirty feet into Fluted Dome, which is two hundred and fifty feet high, fluted on all sides, with some grand recesses like adjacent domes.

You now return to the Elephant, and pass along Broadway to Cheat Avenue. You soon come to Mark Antony's Pit, over which you pass on a wooden bridge. The Pit is sixty feet deep below you. Above you, when you stand on the bridge, is Cleopatra's Dome, about two hundred feet high. Across the pit, opposite the bridge, is Pompey's Pillar, a grand projection from the side of the dome fifty feet high.

Pass along Grand Entrance Avenue, and you can find your way by a ladder to the bottom of Mark Antony's Pit. The bottom is about ten feet wide and fifty feet long. From this you descend six or eight feet, through a high archway, and going onward one hundred feet, you are in Prison Hall, eight feet wide, one hundred feet long, and fifty feet high.

Return to Mark Antony's Pit, and take Fenn's Avenue. You descend sixteen feet, and then ascend again fourteen feet; you are in Nellie's Chamber, a room eight by fourteen feet, with an arched ceiling. This little grotto is beautifully decorated with a kind of grape work, and crystalized incrustations. You pass down a ladder twelve feet, into Gibbon's Rest, a convenient stopping place.

You now begin to enter upon the Ruins of Palmyra. You climb over and clamber among a shapeless mass of fallen rocks for several rods. The walls of the avenue and their projections strikingly resemble the ruins of some ancient city.

Here you enter Duncan's Avenue, and immediately upon your right is Boone's Monument, a pillar of stone ten feet through and twenty feet high. Around the top is an elegant cornice of stone, and the whole monument is beautifully decorated with calcareous globules, from the size of a pin head to that of a hickory nut, attached to the column by a slender stem of stone.

Following Duncan's Avenue, you are soon in a tight place. If you are a man of good size, just lay off your coat, vest and hat;

then squeeze yourself through a very narrow channel in the rocks for a rod or two, crawling part of the time. The rocks on both sides of you are thickly studded with globular projections and sharp points like those on Boone's Monument, and render your ingress next to impossible.

But you have got through and are now in the Cathedral, and feel richly repaid for your toil. See those grand arches and that rich ornamental work, far away above your head. Look also at those beautiful recesses in the walls, room enough for the images of nearly all the saints in the calendar. Whence came that Fallen Pillar at your feet? It was doubtless once a part of the grand framework above.

Take now a little avenue and pass up it one hundred feet and you are in the Vestry Room, about twelve feet across and thirty feet high.

You now return to Boone's Monument and

take Duncan's Avenue again. This is a grand passage. It is lofty and the sides consist of splendid columns which unite in a lofty arch above your head. A walk of a dozen rods brings you to Black Donald's Pit, and you enter it at the bottom. It is circular and about fifteen feet across. From this you ascend a ladder twenty- six feet and stand at the entrance of Wool's Avenue. Stop now and look back to the other side of the pit. There is a projection from the side exactly resembling an old fashioned Pulpit, a semi-circular prominence, the Bible-cushion being a layer of flint. Over the pit is a dome seventy-five feet high.

Advancing for a dozen rods through Wool's Avenue, you stand at Capitola's Trap.* You ascend a ladder twenty-three feet through a perpendicular hole only three feet in diameter and escape out of the top of the trap.

---

* These names were borrowed by Mr. Peddicord from Mrs. Southworth's story of the Hidden Hand.

Now you are in Hurricane Avenue, a winding passage, which by a gentle descent leads you back to Wall Street, and you pass along it again to Dripping Dome, under which is Kellion's Pit. You pass over the pit on a bridge and enter Pine Apple Avenue. Right by your side and above you are the most perfect representations of pine apples in stalactite, the apples a foot or two long. These are very beautiful. There, too, is a stalagmite Pyramid, eight feet through at the base, and six feet high. A crown of stalactites is twenty feet above you, and in the solid rock near you is set a magnificent collection of quartz crystals, called the Snowdrop Crystals.

From this point you return to the mouth of the cave, after a journey of seven or eight miles among the subterranean grandeurs. Yet you have not explored all these mysterious avenues.

What a field is here opened for the skill of the artist's pencil! What delineations of grandeur could here be made! Will not some one of adequate skill undertake the work, and reveal to the world in their true forms these scenes of beauty and sublimity which have so long been hidden from human view?

A visit to this cave is well worth a long pilgrimage. Its attractions are of a different kind from those of Diamond and Mammoth Caves.

The Diamond Cave excels in the exquisite beauty of its formations. The Mammoth Cave excels in its vast extent, and the Hundred Dome Cave excels in the variety, grandeur and sublimity of its scenery.